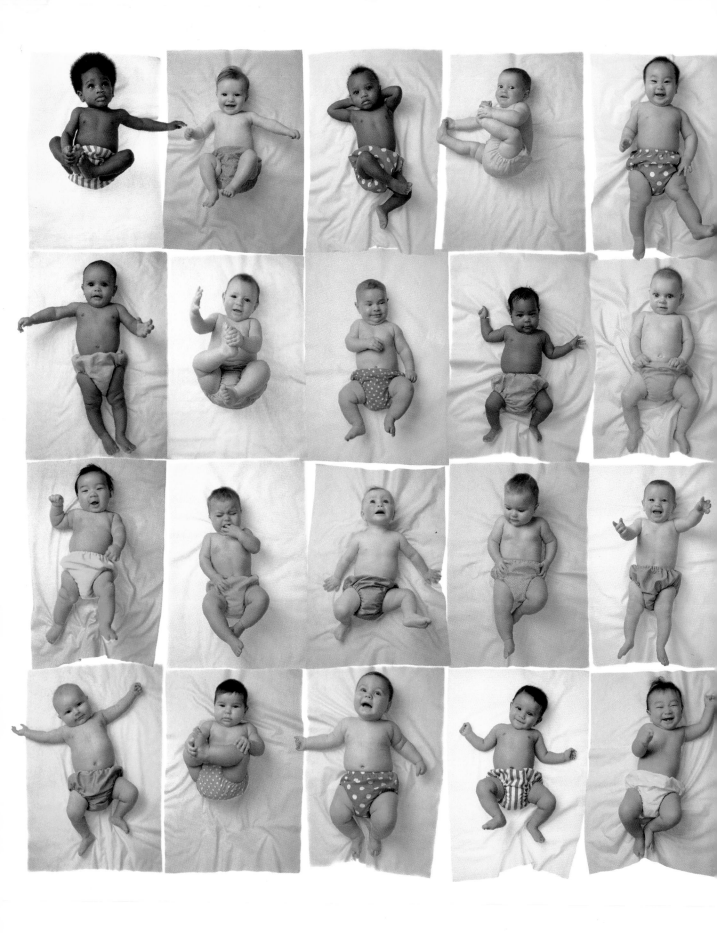

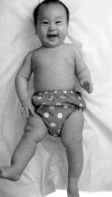
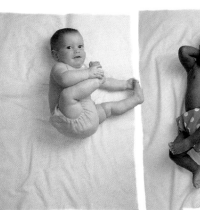

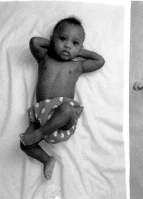

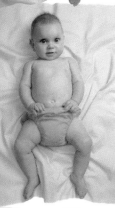
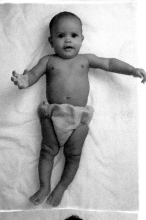

WOW!
BABiES!

Penny Gentieu

Crown Publishers, Inc.
New York

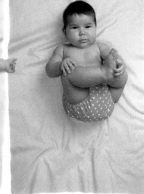
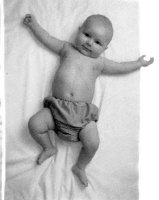

Hellooo... babies!

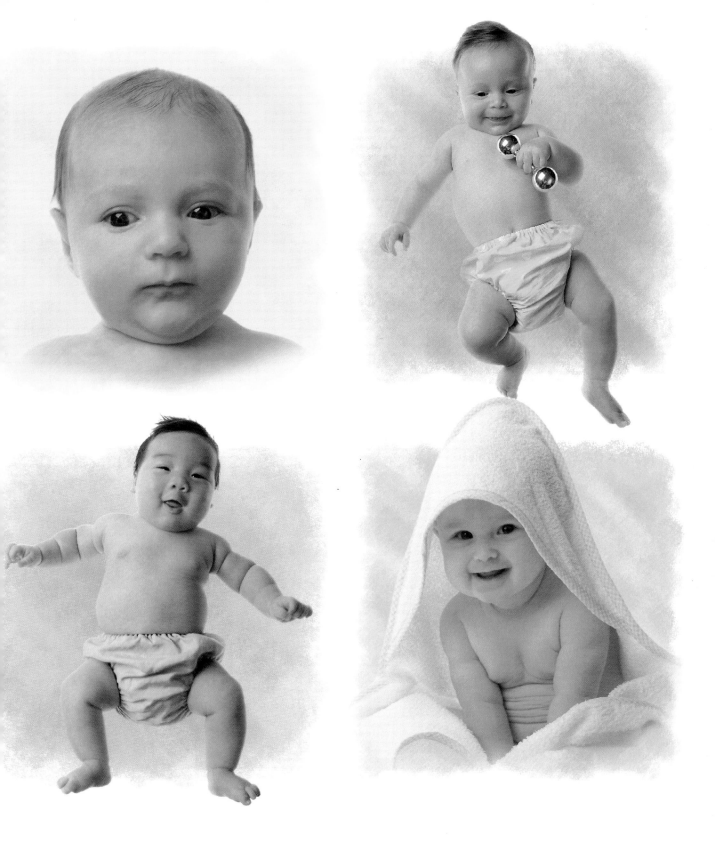

HAPPY babies

Hungry babies

Busy

babies

pretty **babies**

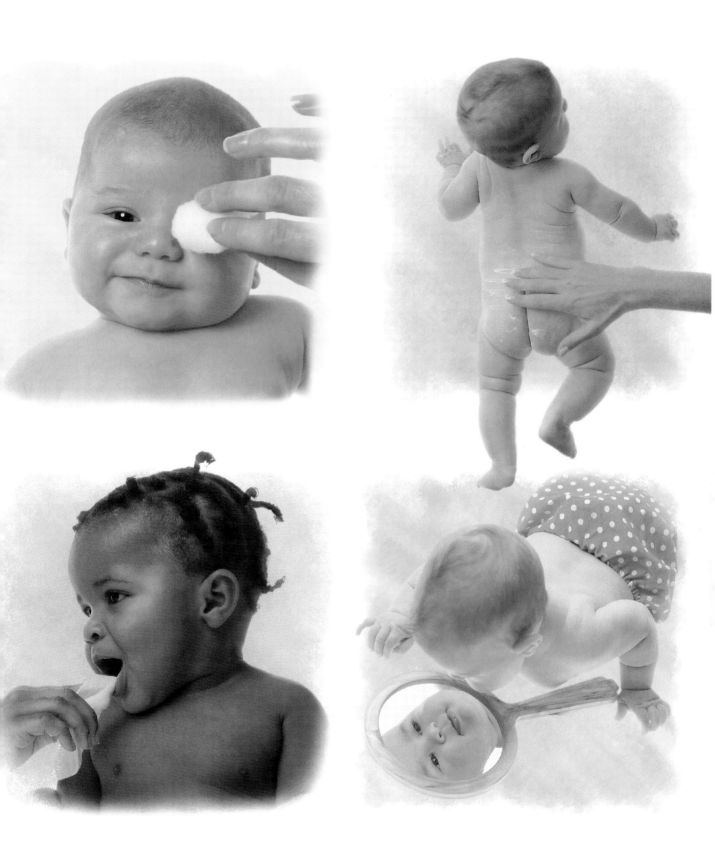

CRYbabies

Hug babies &

kiss babies

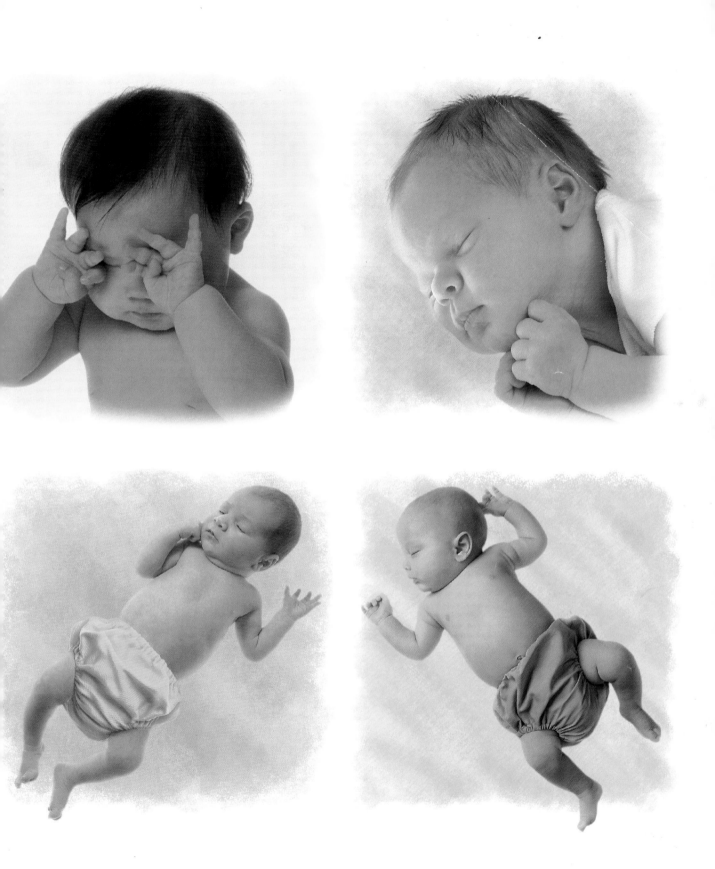

Night-night, babies.

For Tom
and our sweet Anna

Published by Crown Publishers, Inc.,
a Random House company, 201 East 50th Street,
New York, New York 10022
CROWN is a trademark of Crown Publishers, Inc.

http://www.randomhouse.com/

Printed in Mexico

Library of Congress Cataloging-in-Publication Data

Gentieu, Penny.
Wow! Babies! / Penny Gentieu
p. cm.
Summary: A collection of photographs displaying
human babies in a wide range of moods
and situations.
[1. Babies—Fiction.] I. Title.
PZ7.G2918Wo   1997
[E]—dc21   97-5344

ISBN 0-517-70963-5 (hardcover)

10 9 8 7 6 5 4 3 2 1

First Edition